NATIONAL GEOGRAPHIC

# Ladders

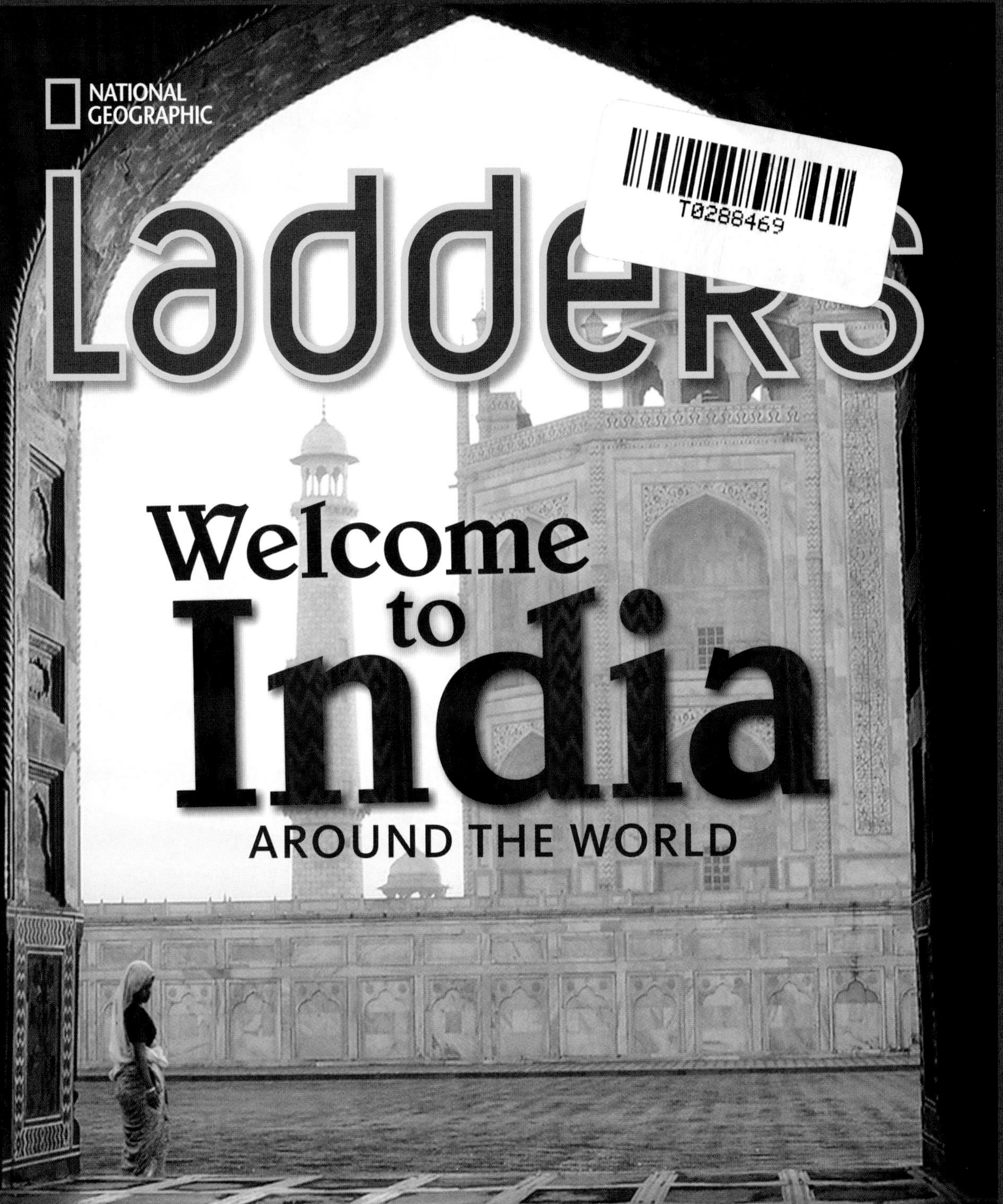

# Welcome to India

## AROUND THE WORLD

# WELCOME TO INDIA

*by Stephanie Herbek*

*Namaste!* That's how people in India say "hello." India is a large country on the continent of Asia. It has mountains, rivers, and deserts. Over one billion people live in India.

**Culture** is important to people in India. Culture includes the food, beliefs, music, art, and language of a group of people. It also includes where a person lives. Culture can be different in small communities and big communities.

> In India, people ride animals alongside cars and trucks. Elephants are a good thing to ride. They have a lot of trunk space!

# Small Villages and Big Cities

Most people in India live in small communities called **villages**. Indian villages have simple homes. There are wide-open spaces to work, farm, and play. Many people live in India's large cities, too. These cities are busy, crowded communities. Life in an Indian village can be different from life in an Indian city.

Sometimes people from villages travel to the cities to buy or sell things. People from cities often go into villages to visit friends. Let's find out more about the villages and cities of amazing India!

# Living in a Village

Indian villages are in the country. They are usually made up of small homes built of mud, straw, and stone. Most village homes don't have electricity, running water, or TV. People in Indian villages fill their water buckets from a **well**. Sometimes there are a few stores and a post office in the village. There might even be a café where people can sip tea with their neighbors.

Many villagers are farmers. They grow crops such as rice and wheat to eat and sell. Lucky villagers might also own a buffalo that gives them milk. Sometimes these buffalo live in the house. That's a big pet!

This fishing village is near the water. Check out the colorful boats and homes.

In a village, people start their busy days early. They fill their water buckets at the well, gather wood for the fire, and cook the morning meal. Then most children head off to small village schools. Some children don't go to school. They work on their family's farm instead. At the end of the day, all village children come together to play.

In this village, children play near homes made of wood and grass.

# Living in a City

India also has some of the most crowded cities in the world. Over ten million people live in Mumbai (muhm-BY). This loud, exciting city has highways and tall, modern buildings. Most Indians who live in cities like Mumbai live in small apartments in big buildings. Many of them work in offices and factories. They do not have space to grow their own food, so they buy it in markets.

> In busy Indian cities, people buy their food at outdoor markets.

Most families in Mumbai live in apartment buildings.

Cities in India have parks, museums, restaurants, and hotels. Many people ride buses or bicycles to get from place to place. They also take the train. Train tracks cover India, moving people from villages to cities and back again.

**Check In** How is living in a city in India different from living in a village?

**Read to find out** about going to school in India.

# Going to School in India

*by Grant Williams*

Children in India get to school in many different ways. In cities, children often hop on the bus to get to school. But children in villages have a trickier time. Mountains, rivers, and forests sometimes stand between children and their schools. Some children ride boats across rivers and tiptoe along swaying bridges just to get to school.

> This boy gets a ride to school each day on his father's bike.

Some Indian schools might surprise you. Teachers teach and children learn in some unusual places. In small villages, a class might be held outdoors. In parts of India that are in the desert, school could be held in a tent. In crowded cities, some students even attend classes inside a parked bus.

Many children walk to school in India. Others think it's more fun to run!

Coming through! These children get pulled to school in a little cart.

It's the rainy season! These girls have to wade through flooded streets to get to school.

# Learning and Playing

Once they get to school, children are ready to learn. They study math, science, and art. They also learn to speak Hindi and English. These are the most important languages in India. Many people in India speak Hindi, but learning English makes it easy for Indians to talk to people around the world. It also helps them understand what life is like in other countries.

In some Indian classrooms, children sit on the floor instead of at desks.

Like children in the United States, children in India exercise during the school day. Many children like to play **cricket** and soccer. Cricket is a sport like baseball, played on a large field with a ball and a bat. You probably already know what soccer is. It's a popular sport all over the world!

Small chalkboards, or slates, make it easy to practice writing words in English.

At recess, some children play games with marbles.

Wearing a uniform is usually part of going to school in India.

# Lunchtime!

Hungry students can't wait for lunchtime. So, what's for lunch in India? Indian farmers grow rice, wheat, peas, and beans in the rich soil. Indian children eat many foods made with these ingredients. Spices, such as **curry**, are often used to flavor dishes of vegetables or meat served with rice. Chili peppers add some spicy flavor to Indian foods, too.

> These children are enjoying their lunch.

Many children in India carry their lunches in a metal lunch box called a *tiffin*. They pack many different foods. Indian people do not eat very much meat. It can be expensive and hard to find. So most children bring rice dishes to school. *Shahi paneer* is a mixture of cheese and vegetables that many children like to eat. Indian children also bring a bottle of water to school. Not all schools have running water.

Kids can carry their lunches to school in tiffins.

*Naan* bread is round, flat, and very tasty.

This delicious curry is made with spicy vegetables and rice.

# No School Today!

In India, as in other countries, children sometimes miss school to celebrate important holidays. Children might celebrate by going to parties, eating special foods, and spending time with their family and friends.

Diwali (dih-WAH-lee) is one of the most important **festivals** in India. It is celebrated in October or November. Diwali is known as "the festival of lights." During Diwali, people light candles in their homes. Colorful fireworks brighten the night sky. It is a happy time of year.

^ Children celebrate Holi by throwing colorful powders at their friends.

Another important festival in India is called Holi (HOH-lee). Holi takes place in March or April and lasts for five days. Holi celebrates the arrival of spring. Just look at all of those colors! In fact, Holi means "the festival of colors." During Holi, people pray and eat special foods. They throw handfuls of colorful powders at each other. What a fun way to celebrate!

**Check In** What are some of the different ways students get to school in India?

**GENRE Folk Tale** **Read to find out** how rumors get started.

# The Foolish, Timid Rabbit

## A TRADITIONAL INDIAN FOLK TALE

*retold by Jenny Loomis*
*illustrated by David Mottram*

Many children's stories contain lessons about life and culture. Jataka tales are one way that children in India learn **morals**, or beliefs about right and wrong. These ancient stories come from Buddhism. This is a religion that started in India 2,500 years ago. The moral in this tale is about the danger of telling **rumors**. As you read this folk tale, think about the lessons that it teaches. Do they sound familiar to you?

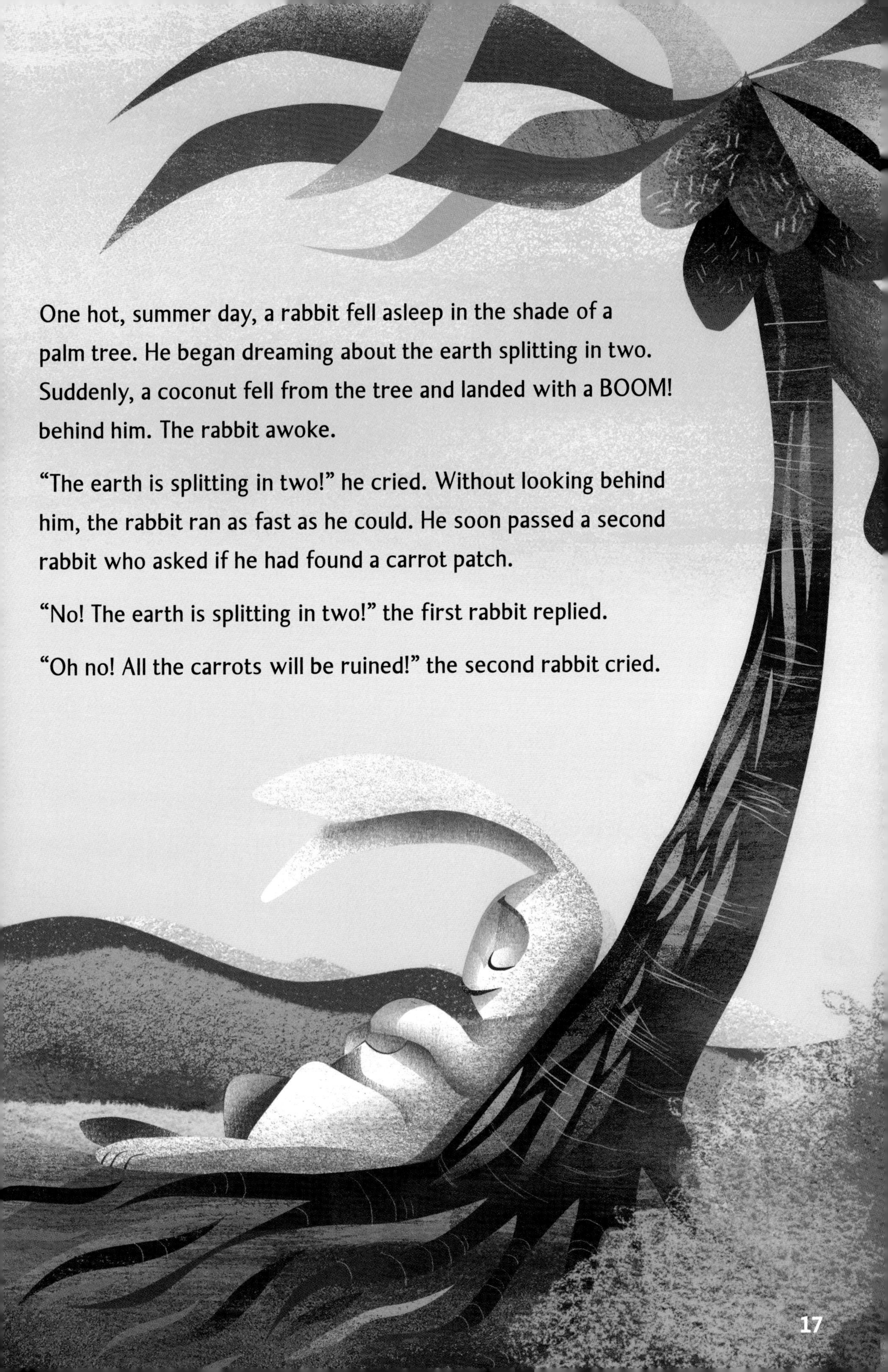

One hot, summer day, a rabbit fell asleep in the shade of a palm tree. He began dreaming about the earth splitting in two. Suddenly, a coconut fell from the tree and landed with a BOOM! behind him. The rabbit awoke.

"The earth is splitting in two!" he cried. Without looking behind him, the rabbit ran as fast as he could. He soon passed a second rabbit who asked if he had found a carrot patch.

"No! The earth is splitting in two!" the first rabbit replied.

"Oh no! All the carrots will be ruined!" the second rabbit cried.

The second rabbit ran to catch up with the first rabbit. The two of them raced through a field. They passed rabbit after rabbit and explained to each that the earth was splitting in two. Soon, hundreds of rabbits were running.

They ran past a monkey who was sitting in a tree, eating a banana. "Rabbits! Rabbits! Where are you going?" he asked. They told the monkey that the earth was splitting in two.

"What will happen to my bananas?" cried the monkey. He swung down from the tree to join them.

The rabbits and the monkey raced past an elephant who asked about the fuss. When the monkey explained that the earth was splitting in two, the elephant said, “How awful! This can’t be good for the plants and trees!” He joined the other animals. Then the animals entered a wooded area where they passed a deer snacking on some moss.

“What on earth is going on?” asked the deer.

“What on earth is right!” answered the elephant. “The earth is splitting in two!”

“Oh my! I hope the moss won’t get hurt!” The deer ran to the front of the line of animals.

The lion, King of Beasts, saw the long line of running animals from the top of a hill and became worried. He ran to the foot of the hill and let out a mighty roar. The animals stopped because they knew better than to disobey him. The lion ordered the animals to explain themselves.

"The earth is splitting in two!" the animals yelled together.

"How do you know this?" asked the lion.

"I think the elephant knows," said the deer.

"You may want to check with the monkey," said the elephant.

"Ask the rabbits! They are the ones who told me!" said the monkey. The rabbits looked at one another.

"Who started all of this?" roared the lion.

The first rabbit timidly raised his paw and explained that he was the one who first found out about the earth. He described the sound he heard while napping under the palm tree.

"Show me where this happened. The rest of you wait here," ordered the lion.

The rabbit ran back to the palm tree with the lion close behind.

"This is it, King Lion! This is where it happened."

The lion looked at the area near the palm tree very carefully. It was not long before he saw the coconut.

"Foolish little rabbit, the earth isn't splitting in two. The BOOM! you heard was the sound of this coconut falling from its tree. Let's go back to the others and explain what happened before there's another stampede."

Upon returning to the hill, the lion explained to the nervous animals that the earth would stay in one piece. The animals started cheering.

"But from now on, check to make sure a rumor is true before acting on it," ordered the lion.

All the animals thought this was a smart plan. They thanked the lion for his wisdom and help. If it wasn't for him, they might still be running.

**Check In** What lesson does this folk tale teach?

## Discuss

1. Tell about some of the ways you think the three selections in this book are linked.

2. Do most people in India live in small villages or in big cities? Which place would you rather live? Why?

3. Which Indian festival is similar to a holiday or festival that you celebrate? How is it similar?

4. Do you think the first rabbit in the folk tale acted foolishly? What makes you think that?

5. What do you still wonder about the land and people of India?